PaRragon

Bath • New York • Singapore • Hong Kong • Cologne • Delhi • Melbourne

HOW TO USE YOUR TRANSFERS

Use your transfers!

INSIDE THIS POWER RANGERS TRANSFER BOOK YOU WILL FIND A SHEET OF TRANSFERS. USE THESE PICTURES TO COMPLETE THE SCENES, ACTIVITIES, PUZZLES AND QUIZZES WHENEVER YOU SEE THE TRANSFER SYMBOL ON THE PAGE.

1. Place the transfer sheet colourful-side up on the page. Make sure your chosen transfer is in the correct position.

2. Firmly scribble over the top of the transfer with a ballpoint pen.

3. Carefully peel back the clear sheet to reveal your transfer!

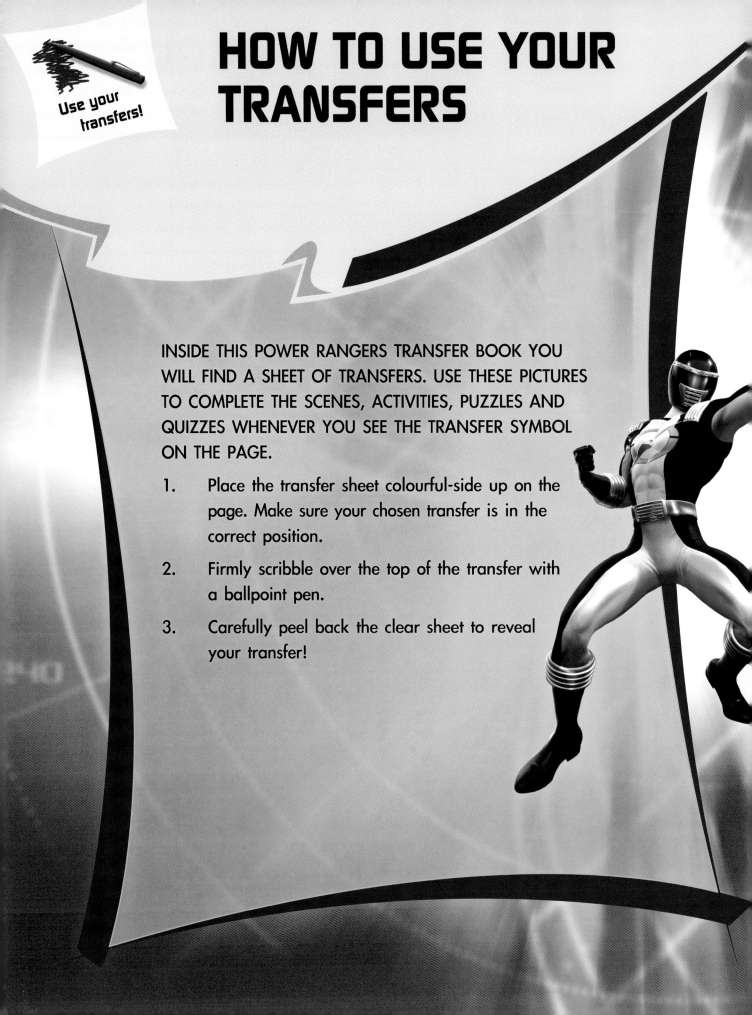

ALL ABOUT ME

MY NAME IS: _____

I AM _____ YEARS OLD.

I LIVE IN: _____

MY FAVOURITE THING TO DO IS:

_____

MY FAVOURITE POWER RANGER IS:

_____

MY FAVOURITE POWER RANGER VEHICLE IS:

_____

MATCH THE SHADOW

The Power Rangers unite to become the ultimate force for good – the Megazord.
Can you see which shadow matches him exactly?

SHADOW 1

SHADOW 2

SHADOW 3

MAZE

Help the Red Ranger find his way through this maze so he can battle the villainous Moltor!

ANSWER ➡

SUDOKU

USE YOUR RANGER POWERS OF REASONING AND LOGIC TO CRACK THIS
MEGA-HARD SUDOKU PUZZLE!

Every row must contain a picture of each of the images below, so must
every column and every square. Use your Power Ranger transfers to fill in
the missing images in the blank spaces. Remember, an image cannot
appear in the same row, column or square twice!

Use your transfers!

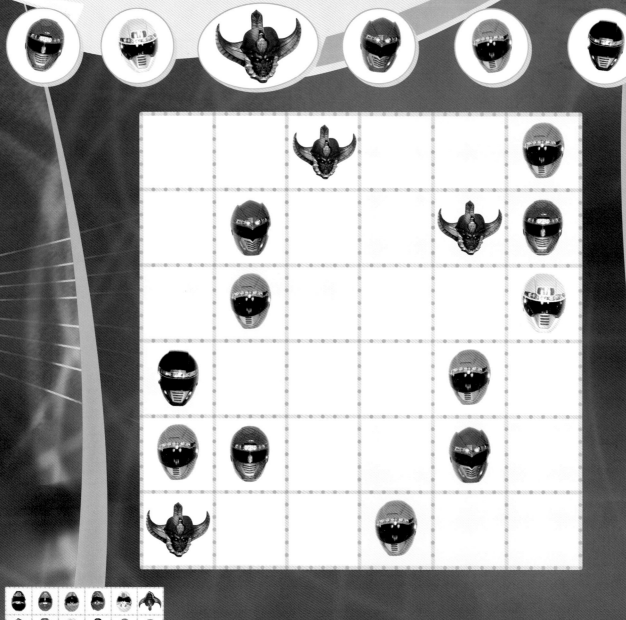

ANSWER

WORD SEARCH

Look up, down, forwards, backwards and diagonally to find these words in the grid below!

MORPHER   JEWEL   INVISIBILITY   ZORD BAY   SHIELD   CROWN

U	Q	Y	A	R	U	Z	J	W	D	S	I
J	A	R	Z	F	J	X	H	E	F	N	R
H	S	E	X	V	M	C	G	R	V	A	E
G	D	H	S	T	I	S	H	I	E	L	D
T	E	P	W	G	K	V	S	T	G	Q	G
R	R	R	E	B	O	I	F	Y	H	W	J
F	Z	O	R	D	B	A	Y	U	N	E	U
D	G	M	D	I	L	B	D	I	W	D	B
S	H	O	L	E	W	E	J	P	O	S	F
E	V	I	C	Y	P	N	S	O	R	A	K
W	T	M	V	H	M	L	A	L	C	X	S
Y	B	J	F	N	H	K	Q	K	J	C	V

ANSWER ➡

COLOUR THIS PAGE IN!

DRIVE MAX ZORDS - TIME TO MOVE OUT!

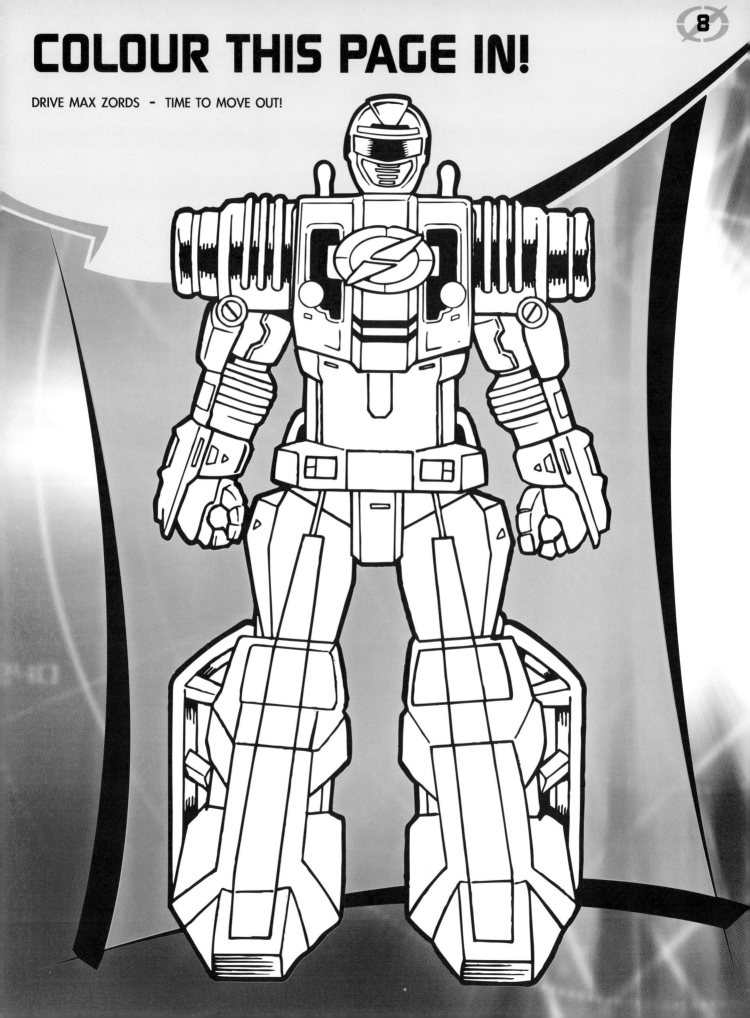

WHICH LINE LEADS TO...

The Black Ranger must use his super powers of sight to lead him to the evil Moltor.
Only then can he battle his enemy and save the world from evil!
Which line will lead him to Moltor?

CODE BREAKER

The seven jewels of power were hidden around the globe to protect them from great evil.
Can you decrypt the code below and reveal the name of one of the missing jewels?

BLACK LIGHT SECRET CODE

___ ___ ___

___ ___ ___ ___ ___

___ ___ ___ ___ ___

A	@
C	©
E	e
H	✦
K	☹
L	☺
P	⊕
R	®
T	▲
U	⊕
Y	▷

UNSCRAMBLE THE WORDS

The Zord bay is hidden in a secret location.
Unscramble the words below to reveal where it can be found.

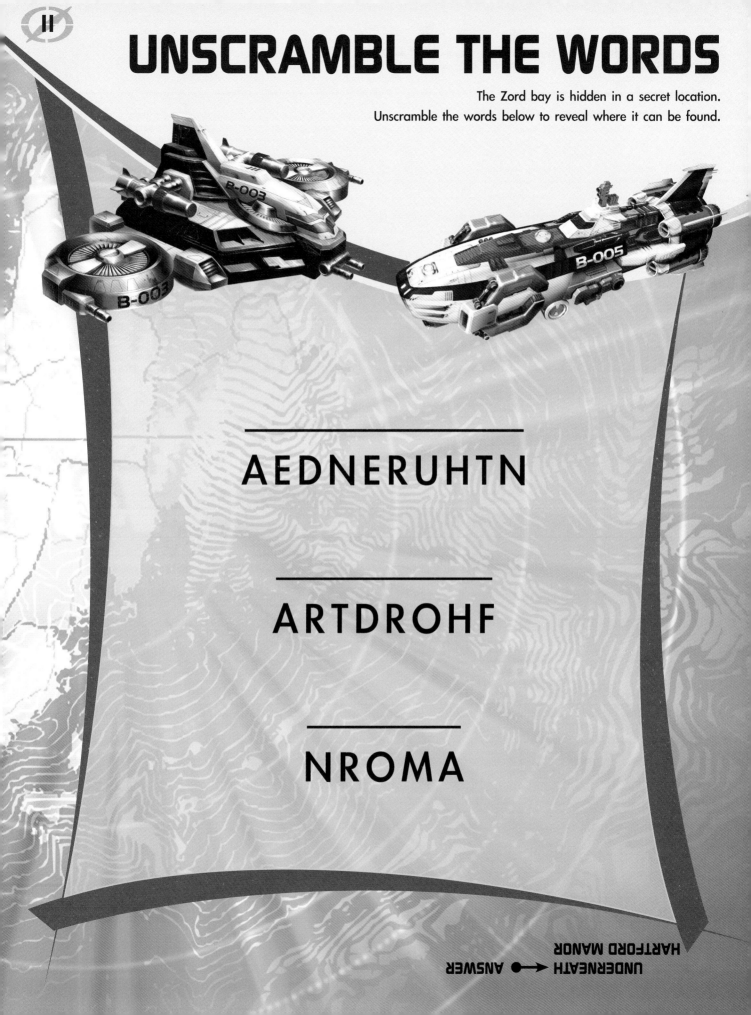

AEDNERUHTN

ARTDROHF

NROMA

COLOUR THIS PAGE IN!

Power Rangers Operation Overdrive use their arsenal of weapons
to destroy the evil brothers Flurious and Moltor.

COUNT THE CHILLERS

Chillers are the evil henchmen of Flurious; they live in
The Ice Den and cold blood runs through their veins!
How many Chillers can you count on this page?

USE A GRID TO DRAW A PICTURE.

Can you copy this picture of the Red Ranger into the grid below?

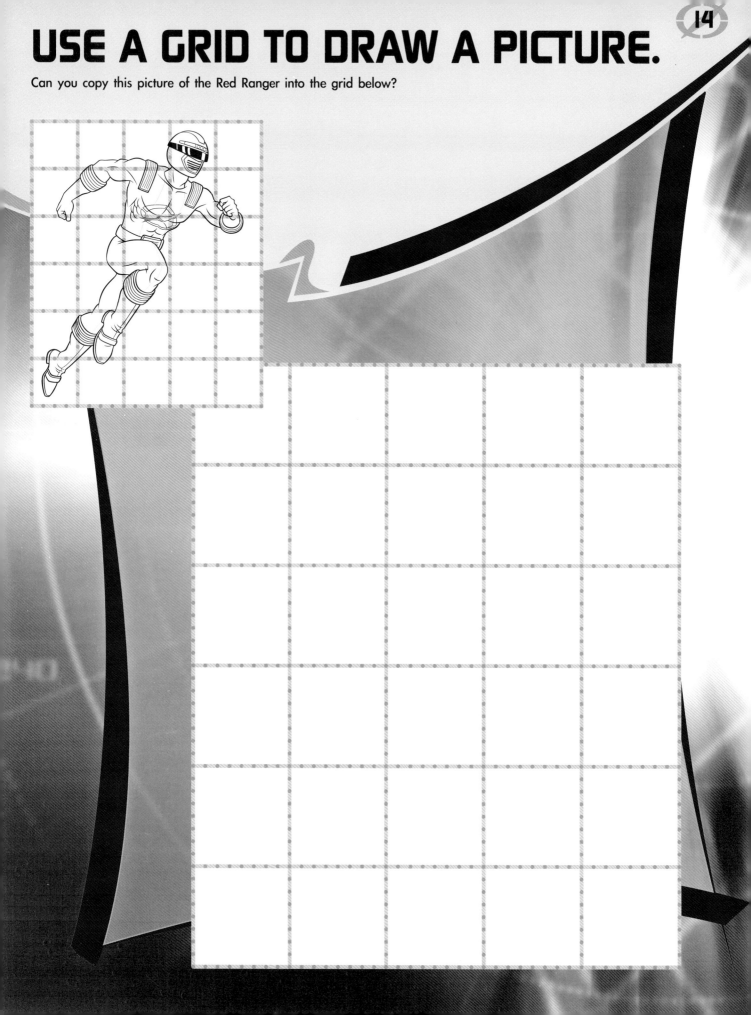

COMPLETE THE SEQUENCE

Use the images from your Ranger transfer sheet
to complete the sequences below.

Use your transfers!

1

2

3

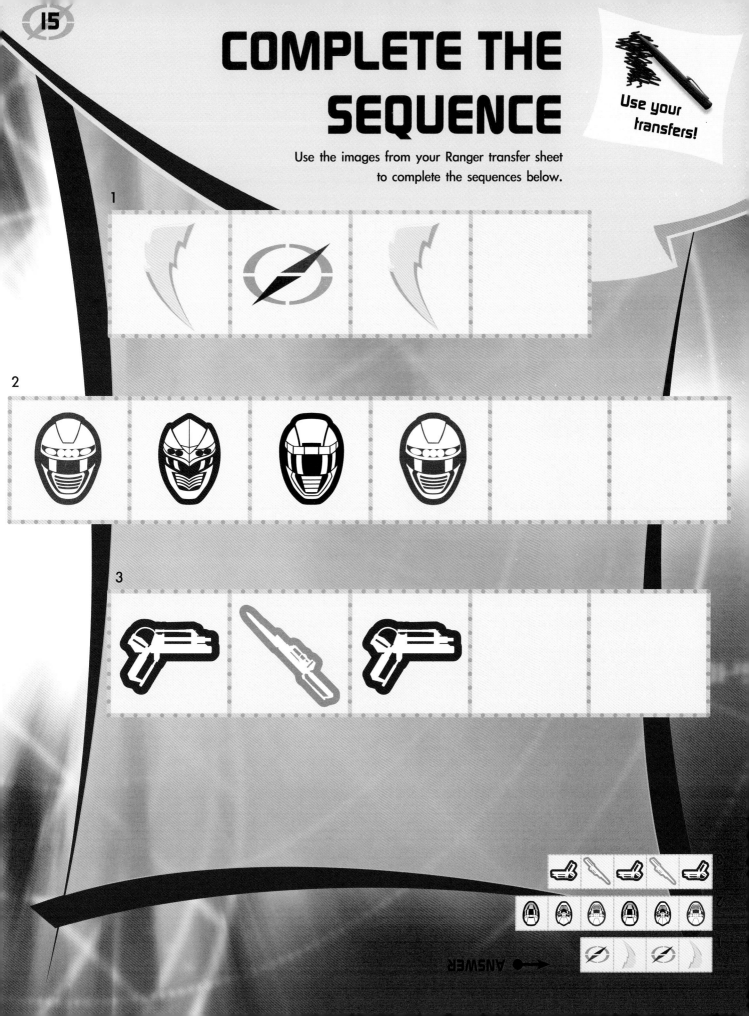

BOARDGAME

Use your transfers and small pieces of card to create counters for this mega-cool game. Take turns with your friends to roll a dice and move around the board. Whoever gets to the end first is the winner!

Use your transfers!

Beware Kamdor! Remain in this square until you roll a six.

You gain Zord power, move forward five squares!

You must wait for Ranger back up. Wait here until you roll a two.

Your path is blocked by molten lava, miss a turn.

START

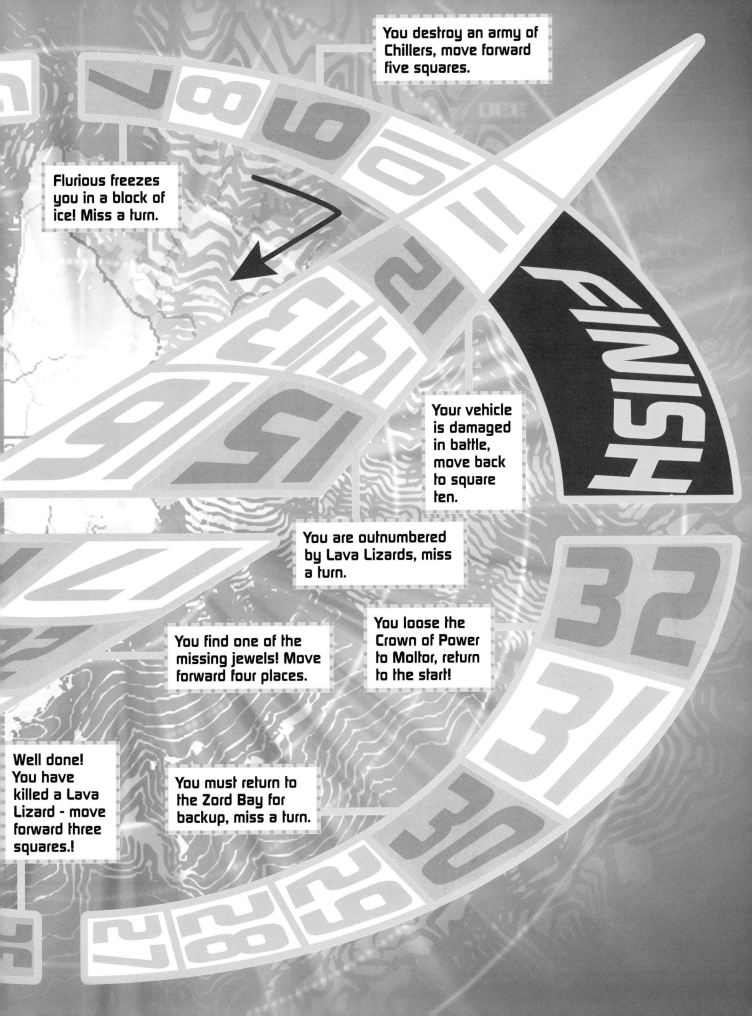

MAKE AS MANY WORDS AS YOU CAN USING THE LETTERS FROM

OPERATION OVERDRIVE.

GOOD VS EVIL.

Our heroes come to the scene to fight!

Black Hovertek Cycle

FOLLOW THE CIRCLE TO CRACK THE CODE.

Overdrive Trekkers help the gang morph into Power Rangers. To find out what the secret code to activate the Trekkers is, go around the circle in a clockwise direction starting at the top and write every other letter in the spaces below.

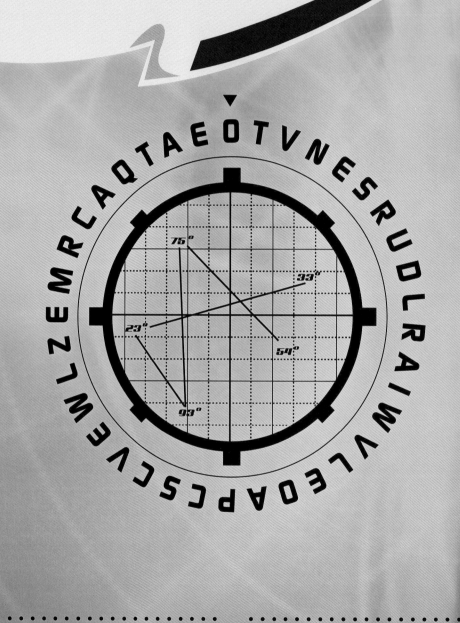

SPOT THE DIFFERENCE

Can you spot the five differences between these two pictures?

ANSWER ➡

FILL IN THE GAPS

Use your expert Ranger knowledge to fill in the gaps in the sentences below.

1) BLACK POWER RANGER'S SUPER POWER IS

_____ _____ ____ _____ .

2) INSIDE THE CORONA AURORA

FIT _____ JEWELS.

3) FLURIOUS IS THE BROTHER OF _____ .

4) THE CROWN OF POWER IS
ALSO KNOWN AS

____ _____

_____ .

MAZE

The evil Flurious has trapped the Megazord within a deadly maze, can you lead him out of it?

START ●→

COLOUR THIS PAGE IN!

Dark forces leave evil where they roam and the responsibility of protecting the galaxy falls to the Power Rangers!

FIND A MATCHING PAIR

Can you spot which two Power Ranger heads make an identical pair?

1

2

3

4

6

5

CROSS WORD

Can you guess the answers to this crossword puzzle? Use the clues below to help you.

ACROSS 1) The evil henchmen of Moltor, whose names begin with 'L'.
      2) This villain is the leader of the Miratrix and was trapped within a crystal for years!
      3) These icy creatures do the bidding of the evil Flurious.

DOWN 4) This wicked creature, whose name begins with 'M', can withstand lava.
      5) The name of the place that the evil Moltor and his henchmen live.
      6) This villain is the brother of Moltor.

CODE BREAKER

Operation Overdrive ride many powerful vehicles into battle. Can you crack the code below and write down the name of the vehicle they must use when their adventures take them to sea?

BLACK LIGHT SECRET CODE

A	15
C	2
D	6
E	10
H	1
I	11
K	16
L	5
N	12
O	3
P	9
R	7
S	14
T	4
U	8
Y	13

___ _____

4 1 10   14 8 9 10 7

_____ _____

1 13 6 7 3   7 10 2 3 12

_____

2 15 7 7 11 10 7

B-005

NAME THE WEAPON

The Power Rangers have many weapons, which they use to fight off evil. Can you name the weapons pictured below?

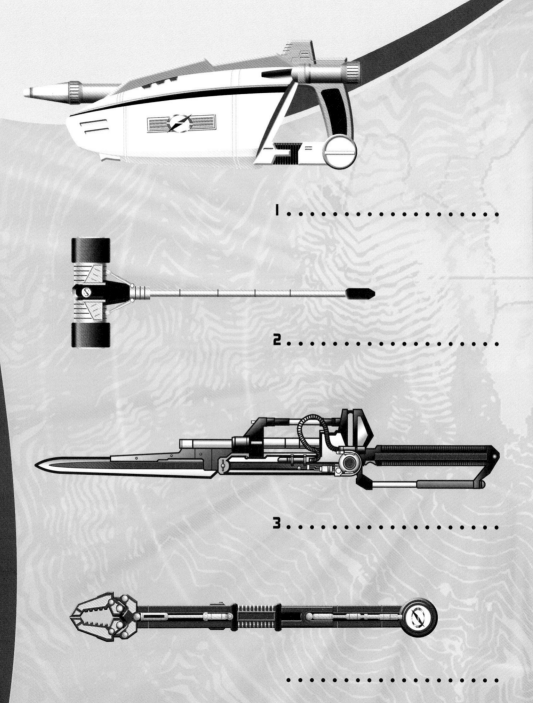

1 . . . .

2 . . . .

3 . . . .

. . . .

SUDOKU

USE YOUR RANGER POWERS OF REASONING AND LOGIC
TO CRACK THIS MEGA-HARD SUDOKU PUZZLE!

Every row must contain a picture of each of the images below. So
must every column and every square. Use your Power Ranger transfers to fill
in the missing images in the blank spaces. Remember, an image cannot
appear in the same row, column or square twice!

Use your transfers!

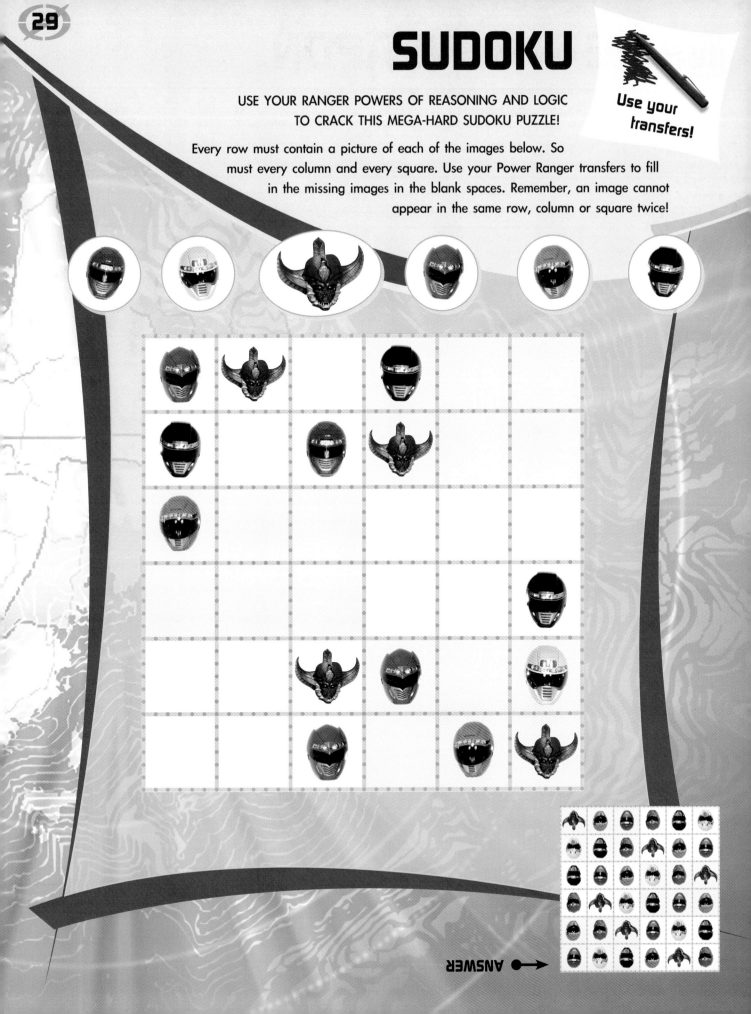

ANSWERS ➡

WORD SEARCH

Look up, down, forwards, backwards and diagonally to find these words in the grid below!

RANGER   STRENGTH   MEGA ZORD   STRIKER   MOLTOR   FLURIOUS

H	T	R	V	D	K	Y	Z	F	A	N	J
P	T	J	R	V	B	R	W	T	J	I	K
A	U	W	A	O	W	S	R	T	E	E	J
S	Y	S	N	U	X	E	Q	V	C	S	F
X	T	F	G	T	K	M	S	D	G	U	B
D	G	K	E	I	C	E	D	E	P	O	J
C	S	T	R	E	N	G	T	H	A	I	L
F	K	T	S	J	B	A	B	Y	G	R	D
V	S	L	F	N	F	Z	N	H	D	U	Y
N	C	R	O	T	L	O	M	K	B	L	Z
Y	V	P	C	G	J	R	J	L	N	F	Q
U	S	I	M	D	Y	D	I	A	U	N	I

◀●━ ANSWER

COLOUR THIS PAGE IN!

Many centuries ago, Flurious and his brother, Moltor, tried to steal the Corona Aurora. But the crown cursed and disfigured them!

UNSCRAMBLE THE WORDS.

Unscramble the words below to reveal what the Power Rangers must search for.

_____
EVNES

_____
LEWSEJ